Poems, Prayers and Unfinished Promises

Gary Allison Furr

Mossy Creek Press

Poems, Prayers and Unfinished Promises
ISBN 978-1-949888-19-5 Softcover
Copyright © 2015 by Gary Allison Furr

All rights reserved. No part of this book may be reproduced or transmitted in any form or by any means, electronic or mechanical, including photocopying, recording, or by any information storage and retrieval system, without permission in writing from the publisher.

Cover design and picture by Gary Allison Furr

To order additional copies of this book, contact:

Mossy Creek Press
1-423-475-7308
www.mossycreekpress.com

Mossy Creek Press is an imprint of Parson's Porch & Company (PP&C) in Cleveland, Tennessee. PP&C is an innovative organization which raises money by publishing books of noted authors, representing all genres. Profits from publishing are shared with the students of Carson – Newman University through its scholarship fund.

*Poems, Prayers
and Unfinished Promises*

DEDICATED TO MY FAMILY
And to
THE PEOPLE OF
VESTAVIA HILLS BAPTIST CHURCH
Without each of whom this book would never have been.

Table of Contents

1. Introduction   9

2. The God of Surprises   *Advent*   11

    Advent
    Come to My Heart, Jesus
    Change Us, O God
    Horizon-Seeking
    Zechariah
    Joy to the World
    Shepherd's Watch
    The Hanging of the Greens
    The Lord Has Come
    This Christmas Eve

3. Tentmaker's Hike   *Epiphany*   31

    Tentmaker's Hike
    Diogenes
    Living Decisively
    Calling
    I Heard the Trees
    More
    A Prayer for Truth
    Seeking God's Call
    The Bounty of Creation
    Instruments of Peace

4. Call and Response   *Lent*   45

    A Prayer for the Beginning of Lent
    He'll Carry You Through
    A Song in Our Heart
    A Prayer for Facing Ourselves
    Being Present
    Weeping With Jesus
    The Journey of Lent
    Cultivating the Lives of Children
    Unraveling
    Farewell Baby Girl

A Prayer for Beginning Again
A Prayer for Justice
The Day Alabama Almost Died
Hoppers
A Prayer to Be Still
Clarksville, Tennessee in 1963

5. The Cross Through the Window   *Holy Week*   73

The Cross through the Window
The Minister
The Solid Rock
That Kind of Love
Handel's Messiah
Christ the Song
Words Fail
Forgiveness
Michael
The Power of Surrender
What It Is
Rutter Requiem
In-Between

6. Running From the Tomb   *Easter*   93

Resurrection
Easter
Sky's A-Clearing
After Easter Prayer
Beginning Again
Awakening
People of the Resurrection
I Missed the 1960's
A Blessing for Second Times
Welcome to Regrets

Introduction

So what IS this book? That's a great question. At first, I suppose it could be said that it is a collection of writings, a hodgepodge if you will created but not really belonging to a collection. According to the Online Etymology Dictionary, "hodgepodge" goes back to medieval times and referred to a stew made of items that did not belong together. None of those items were disgusting alone, but collectively, they just didn't work.

Were that to happen here, I would be most disappointed. I have come to think of my writing, my little children of the mind, as one. Many years ago, I began going to a spiritual director, an Episcopal brother trained in the field, spiritually challenging and intuitive about matters divine. I went out of a sense that I needed a person and place where I could bring my life to someone who could help me see what God was up to, one who could give good feedback and call attention to important traces of the divine.

I began to officially journal, though I had been doing so since college. Journaling is ultimately a dismal experience, for a good journal is meant to be burned just after death. This is so that the writer will be utterly honest and it is hard to be so forthright with an audience in one's mind. But it is dismal also because, as one looks back and rereads a journal, the writer is likely to also see that the same handful of limitations, blind spots and preoccupations that were present at the start of life are still there.

During that time, though, much younger and more oblivious even than I still remain, I tended to partition my inner life into various compartments, seeing some as more spiritual than others, some secular or crazy or sinful or useless. My spiritual director friend kept saying and eventually convinced me, that the compartments were all one, the same life, the same truth, lived out before the same God.

Sometimes, in my journaling, I tended to write Henri Nouwen-like, serious and contemplative and that was a good voice. But over the years I was writing lots of other things—songs, because I am a musician, poems, newsletter columns, newspaper articles, academic articles, books and chapters in books.

I noticed something in recent years, though, something very interesting to me. No matter what I write, I have a certain "voice," my voice, or, I would say now, the voice God so kindly gave me. It is not the greatest voice ever, but it is mine and I have learned to be thankful for it. My songwriter friend Pat Terry once said during a seminar on songwriting that "finding your own voice" is crucial to good songwriting. I began to hear this from other songwriters and writers and I believe it is a truth for all lives, whether they ever write or not.

"Finding your voice" is leaving home to begin the quest to find your way back home again. It is a quest to honor your calling, to seek to see your own life as God does. It is terrifying, hopeful and unavoidable.

I would not call this little collection a hodgepodge. It is a map of my journey, back and forth, weaving without knowing the pattern, in the quest for my own voice. They are songs, little poems and pastoral prayers written for congregational settings. They are written over many years, some as early as college and early days in ministry. Others were produced under the fire of weekly demands of ministry, simply because I needed "something" to say. Still others came on me like Jacob's mysterious visitor at the Jabbok and I wrestled all night for a blessing.

I have noticed at this time of my like something wonderful. My spiritual director was right—they are really one, not many. They are mine. I simply share them here in the hope that they might give you, the reader, some inspiration, a chuckle here and there, perhaps a nod of recognition, or simply help you affirm that something is not only your struggle.

But I also offer them as an affirmation that apparently random and unrelated strands in one's life, threads that we seem to work so hard to keep separate early on, begin to weave themselves together as time goes on, sturdy, marvelous evidence of a Power to make us whole in spite of ourselves most of the time.

This book is three "strands" of my life, if you will, but all bound by the medium of writing. Song lyrics, poetry and pastoral prayers are merely different variations of the "one." Whenever you are telling truth, even if to yourself, you aren't far from prayer. Some traditions frown on written prayers, but a prayer can be just as pretentious on the fly as when it is thought about for a while. It's the words used and the occasion that determines how good or bad it is.

This volume is composed of those three strands, put into chapters around the church year. I chose that because a long time ago, I decided to live by the church year, more or less, rather than my own schedule. In part I chose that when I went into the ministry and chose to serve churches.

Each year, more or less, we make the journey of the Great Story. The church year is really simple, if you don't get into all the intricacies of this or that day in some traditions. It is, quite simply, a way to structure the church's time around her story in Scripture. It begins with Advent, the four Sundays before Christmas, leading us from the Old Testament toward the story of Jesus. After this comes Christmastide, then comes Epiphany, the time between Christmas and Lent. The Sundays after "Epiphany Sunday" are sometimes called, "the Sundays after Epiphany." Later comes Lent, Holy Week and Easter, Eastertide, Pentecost and then "ordinary time."

So this is a companion for the year, walking along in the great tradition of pilgrimage. I mean it to be something to pick up and read as you have a moment. It fits nicely for a devotional companion, I suppose, but I didn't construct it that rigorously.

In this volume, I chose only to go from Advent to Easter. Like the disciples in the upper room, it makes sense to sit and wait after something as momentous as a resurrection.

I have to thank more people than there is space to thank—my wife Vickie and family whose love so often inspire me, dear friends and loved ones, Ron DelBene and his wife Eleanor, Fisher and Caroline Humphreys, and my congregations, who called and demanded from me so much of what was written under fire.

I appreciate readers—Fisher, Paul Basden, Paul Robertson, LaRue Speights, Ann Knight, Cynthia Wise, Sheryl Churchill, who read for errors and typos, but bear no guilt for the content. And thanks to David Tullock who is an encourager to writers and an advocate for finding our voices, whether anyone reads them or not. For his sake, I hope they read us.

All good writing is occasional. Something or someone called it into being for some purpose. Even if it isn't that great, it speaks to something. These writings came sometimes from the weekly grind of church, at other times the inspiration of something while I was going about my business.
I am appreciative to the congregation of Vestavia Hills Baptist Church,

whose members support my writing, music and creative urges and affirm me for doing it. I also appreciate my musical friends through the years— Herb Trotman, Glenn Tolbert, Bobby Horton, Brent Warren and especially my bandmates, Greg Womble, Nancy McLemore Womble, Don Wendorf, Paul Wendorf and Melanie Rodgers, for community and inspiration.

The lyrics are mostly from the six albums I've been part of musically and they are available on my website www.gafurr.com or on iTunes and Amazon music.

I hope you like these writings. But I would rather they encourage you to develop your own voice, the one that is weaving in you even now, in the ways that are uniquely yours. The title was inspired, obviously to fans of seventies music, by a music album of John Denver's that I learned to play and loved after I got my twelve string guitar at age 15 for Christmas. The title cut says

> "And talk of poems and prayers and promises
> And things that we believe in
> How sweet it is to love someone
> How right it is to care
> How long it's been since yesterday
> What about tomorrow
> What about our dreams
> And all the memories we share."
>
> *Songwriter: Denver, John (Deutschendorf)*
> *Poems, Prayers And Promises lyrics © Warner/Chappell Music, Inc., Kobalt Music Pub America Inc, Reservoir One Music.*

--Gary Allison Furr

The God of Surprises

Advent

Advent

I truly love Advent and Christmas. I have loved it even more as I learned about the Christian church year. Instead of a month of Christmas, shepherds and schmaltzy cantatas about the nativity, Advent is fullness of time, waiting and hoping against hope. It is learning, annually, not to collapse into despair. This was a pastoral prayer I gave one year at the beginning of the season.

You are the strength of our lives, O God,
and the source of our joy. You are our court of last appeal
and we long for the psalmist's assurance that
"light dawns for the righteous and joy for the upright in heart."
As this, yet another Advent, begins, we pray to find its hope, joy, love and peace.

We pray that those who sow in tears might find hope,
For all those who are like the mothers of Bethlehem
whose children were taken by the evil of the king.
Some have had the joys of earth snatched away by darkness.
So, too, be with mothers in refugee camps and homeless shelters
and mothers who fear their children's future.
Be with men who have no future and lie down wherever they can stay warm.
Be with children who lie down at night, afraid
or hungry or unsafe from predators in their neighborhoods
or in their own house.
Be with those who suffer behind the walls of affluence
While their lives unravel before their eyes.

Like the shepherds
give us the joy of undeserved blessing,
that lifts us out of the dull routine to intersect with providence,
the joy that leads us to Jesus
and sends us away to share the news.
Give us ears to hear and eyes to see your angels,
Bring alive the pages of scripture
Bring us alive so that we might receive them, words become flesh.
And fill our hearts to overflowing with the glory of your deeds.

Like Joseph,
we yearn for the peace of surprising guidance
that charts our way through the deserts.
When our souls dwell in danger and our lives are at risk
you come to us: in dreams and strangers from afar
in circumstances and visions,

in the night and in unexpected moments.
And in your coming, there is always the joyful discovery
that you love us as your children and guide us home.

Like Mary,
give us the bliss of trusting obedience,
that listens quietly when obstinate hearts
might prefer control and anger.
Help us taste the quiet depth of her tranquil heart within our own.
Teach us to treasure in our hearts
when our mouths try to open in complaint or resentment
If we face a terrible truth or some path that leads to a cross
Let our silence be hopeful wonder.

Like Simeon and Anna,
give us the reward of faithful waiting,
As we press up against hard years and barren hopes,
pain that will not subside,
a wrong that will not be righted,
or a prayer that seems never to come true,
As we see signs of decay and despair,
as our nation seems to perish from indifference
and crack from the pressures and transitions of its problems
Teach us to wait with courage
Let the day come when waiting is over
and fulfillment brings shouts that come faster than our words,
because Your kingdom's justice reigns and love prevails.

And finally, like the Holy Family, that the perfect circle of love,
Mother, father and longed for child,
Kept warm in the night by the shelter of each other
Watched over by You,
Could our families be healed in our journeys,
so that fractured dysfunction becomes forgiveness and grace?
Could our love no longer be bartered, conditioned, undelivered
And withheld, damaged and crippled by our histories
And instead, be imitation of the Trinity, perfect circle
Father, Son, Holy Spirit, Three yet One,
Eternal and Everlasting in the heavens?

Such is our Advent prayer
help us to long for nothing else
to accept no cheapened sinful substitutes

and if anything be in the way of Your full joy in us
Grant us the courage to repent and be cleansed
That the highway be opened
for the arrival of the king, Jesus Your Son,
the Joy of our lives. In Whose Name we pray. Amen.

Come to My Heart, Jesus

This was a pastoral prayer during Advent. How can we ask the One who is always with us to "come to us?" I think it is only our way to ask ourselves to come to Him.

Come to my heart, Lord Jesus.
Come?
Why would we ask you to come to a world
Where you lived before I was born?
Why do we talk about "going to the manger"
when the story came and went before us?
You are always here
Your love is always with us
You never leave or forsake us.

And yet, you do not enter without knocking
You graciously wait outside the door of our will and ourselves.
You chose to let us live disconnected if that is what we want

This freedom you gave us is sometimes maddening
Because we do not know how to abide as you do--still, at peace,

With us all is restlessness and unhappiness
anxiety and worry and fear—though you are right there all the time
Our words, "I love you, too" are so important to you
that you leave us to our wandering until we come to ourselves
and say it from our hearts

Help us to see, help us to know
Forgive us for our stubbornness that refuses what we most need.
Repair the damage that breeds suspicious minds
Liberate us to say, "I love you, too,"
when You whisper your tender passion for us
so we might say "I love you, too."
And when we look at the world you love
and see you in the faces of hungry children and wounded souls,
say, "I love you, too" and give ourselves and our means
to say,
Come in.
Come in to my heart, Lord Jesus.
There is room in my heart for you." Amen.

Change Us, O God

Mighty God,
we believe that you are able to speak new things into being,
to create a universe or end it,
call forth a nation or judge it,
set the captives free or permit them to suffer from their own follies.
You are able to sustain the weak,
Redeem the sinner, change the hardened heart
    and call the unlikely.
That being so, we pray with fear and trembling
    in these uncertain times--
Not that you comfort, insulate, give us shortcuts or somehow exempt us
    from life.
We do not ask you to make us into someone else
    Or be just like another in perfect imitation, escape our past
    Or help us ignore its damage.
Do not spare us from our sorrow and grief
    or approve us too easily when we stray
Do not answer us at every call of distress,
and do not rescue us from our own disasters.
Though we may think these things are what we want,
    they leave us less than fully human and essentially unchanged,
    still immature, still broken, still needy and childlike in our souls.
Instead, we pray that you might transform us,
    even as we do not understand the depth of our asking.
Call us past the place of comfort and expertise to a place of deeper faith.
Urge us past familiar people to those who will require deeper love.
Challenge us to persist in times of hardship and difficulty
    so that we might learn to hope and pray and persevere
    to become people who know how to trust you in all things..
This is what we truly need. Then perhaps we will truly believe that
    all sadness will someday melt away,
    all tears will dry,
    all pain will cease,
    all childishness will turn to memory of progress,
    all selfishness will turn to service,
    all our resistance will change to willing obedience born of love.
If this is our destiny, our longing and our true joy,
then help us to find it
and help us to want it enough to seek. In Jesus' name. Amen.

Horizon-Seeking

Have you ever tried to peer over the earth's edge,
where the sky drops off beyond the spot called,
"As Far As the Eye Can See?"
You can walk there all day long if you wish
and you will pass through cities filled with suffering
and desperate efforts to flee them.
You will walk past homes filled with empty pretension
and people with vacant looks in their eyes.
You might run there as though in a marathon,
like those gaunt, sweat-soaked week-end zombies,
You will pass people in all kinds of relentless races,
with all sorts of looks on their faces,
some running full-tilt, some collapsed on the side,
and others disappearing into alleys without a trace,
to push out the hole in their hearts--
the God-made place where the horizons
are supposed to meet . . . .

You will run past the cities and out to the sea,
but the horizon only runs faster away as you seek,
And still the sky and the earth do not join:
not on mountains, or seashores or cities that gleam.

Is it only illusion, this dream of a meeting?
Or must we wait for heaven to fall,
in some unforeseen future by-and-by
like a pine cone seeking some unsuspecting head?
Is this horizon we reach for only apparent, but never meeting,
the hope that dwells in a place called, "Not Yet?"

Zechariah

Old Zechariah is my hero in Advent. Someone I can relate to—hard to trust, dull to visions, can talk about religion all day long, but doesn't take his shoes off for a burning bush and walks right past. Now THERE is a saint I can relate to...

Think for a minute if you can recall
A time when <u>your</u> mouth opened only to stall.
Boiling anger turned into rage,
words and feelings, like a waterfall--
But the best that you could do was sputter,
"WHY...I'LL...YOU...HOW COULD YOU..."
Feelings caged,
lips banging like a broken shutter in the wind.

Good news leaves people speechless, too!
As though you never thought that you
deserved to win or gain applause.
No matter how you worked it through,
A voice inside says, "It's not <u>that</u> good."
There are no words to say because
you weren't prepared to hear a blessing.

Grief can be too great for words
as we peer into the abyss of the absurd.
"Talk about it--you'll feel better," they say,
As you struggle to absorb what has occurred,
but the problem is not that you don't want to talk;

How do you verbalize a hole, a void, an empty space?

There are no words for what is lost or never was.

Gabriel only named the emptiness inside
that left the faithful priest tongue-tied,
a vessel dry and thirsty, yet ill-prepared to drink.
He never said that God's emissary lied;
But custom's well-worn paths within his heart
too-well defined what one might hope or think
and so his road ran off the map and into silence.

Joy to the World

Joy is the craziest, most unwarranted response to life that can be. It is also the most wonderful state of being possible. To have it, I have to stop seeing how I'll look to everyone else, measuring what it will do for me, stop comparing mine to someone else's. Joy requires simply being there. A prayer for Christmas Sunday.

It is morning and we seek you, O Lord.
You said joy comes in the morning.
We have cried enough tears in the night.
We have labored long over our sins and shame,
we face an uncertain future,
and see the disconcerting sight of the tomb
that lays in wait at the end of our way.
We have labored long to make our journey
and met with restlessness and second thoughts.
Anxiety feeds our hunger
and fear increases our thirst.
Sadness weighs upon so many.
Inequities and dark injustice,
sin and degradation mock us.
How can there be joy?

But He has come, Christ the Son,
not into some perfect world, but into this one where we live.
It quickens our hearts,
tears turn to hope again
and death is pushed back from our minds.
Joy pours forth like peals of laughter ringing in our ears.

Christ is born in Bethlehem!   Christ lives with us today!
Christ will one day come again!
And so we sing our praise!
Joy now dwells even in the night, in every broken heart and every lonely soul.
Where Christ comes joy soon follows.

Pour joy upon us,
Drench us with its ecstasy,
Cast out every shred of dignity and reputation
so we might taste one single drop of your full joy
Joy abundant, full of life. Amen.

Shepherd's Watch

My wife, Vickie, was director of a program aimed at getting people back into the workforce and off government assistance. At Christmas one year, she asked me to come and give a devotional for the workers in that area who did this work, mostly helping women who lived lives of desperate poverty, kept there sometimes by the indifference and collusion of those who had what they lacked and who made all the rules. It was hard, frustrating work. And so I wrote this little piece for them, not, as it might appear, for preachers. The shepherds keeping watch over the flocks of God are not only in churches, maybe not primarily there. They are sitting in lonely fields and their work is hard. But it is the work of God.

Among the special list of guests that Holy Night,
the angelic choruses and innkeeper and beasts,
(And later wise men from the east),
were shepherds, doing as shepherds always do--
keeping their flocks in the night.

Sheep are lovable and sweet and warm to the touch,
but they also wander off and so
if one goes toward the cliff the rest
proclaim her queen and over the edge they go.
Their fleece may be as white as snow,
but they're easily fleeced, as shepherds know.
Lost in cold weather sheep have been known
to eat their own fleece; they die with full bellies
and nothing to protect them from the cold.

That's why you are so special, Shepherds of the Weak.
Each day you take your watch over your flock
Through months of discouraging words and tedious tasks,
each day to send these lambs back home
to wolves and lions, bad boyfriends and false shepherds.
No one comes to the hillside to thank you,
Only to see you when one gets away.

That's why shepherds saw the angels and Herod didn't.
Herod saw budgets, threats and turf, nothing more--
babies in the way.
Shepherds know the grass at the roots, so to speak.
Living next to daily risks will do that.
And so the angel chorus welcomed His birth
but it also poured God's blessing out on those
Who sit on hillsides everywhere and faithfully watch.

The Hanging of the Greens

Baptists with liturgy are funny. This started as a poem, just for fun to read for my Pastor's time at the Christmas banquet one year. It got a lot of laughs, even if it is pretty dark. A friend asked me for help to understand the Southern personality. My friend, Herb, says a Southerner is always one of two songs, either "Dublin Blues" by Guy Clark or "Car Wheels on a Gravel Road" by Lucinda Williams. My description is simpler. Our motto is, "Get away from us and leave us the h--- alone. Oh, can y'all come over for supper tomorrow?"

Mostly we are a peaceful folk, down here in the South.
We only turn violent when someone runs their mouth--
If they criticize my football team or tell me what to do
(Well, there WAS that little Civil War) and all our family feuds.

Protestants and Catholics, they never done too well,
believing only they are saved, the others straight to hell.
We Baptists often wonder if the Pope's an antichrist.
Our preachers pray to save us from bingo, wine and vice

But otherwise, you couldn't find more peaceful folk than we.
We're twice as much religious and loan our stuff for free.
If you're a serial killer, we'll have you out to eat.
So I was stunned to hear the news about the hanging of the Greens.

It started when the Catholics started creeping into church,
With acolytes and litanies and little things at first,
called themselves "the Chrismons," someone said to me,
So no surprise one Sunday night they hung 'em on a tree.

It musta' been a ghastly thing, they printed programs, too,
and children all were singing, even as they came to view.
They hung 'em all on Christmas trees, funeral wreaths alight
strung 'em up across the land, hanged with Christmas lights,

Must have hid the bodies up in the heating ducts
I heard 'em mention "Ad-vents" and hauling things in trucks
I imagine it was like no sight you have seen,
the bloody night of murder, the hanging of the Greens.

Years from now great grandchildren will still be singing songs
of Jesse James and Pretty Polly and how Sherman done us wrong,
And we'll add the tale when Baptists across the South one night

gathered in the churches and hanged every Green in sight.

I've tried to tell the Baptists, you can't let this get out,
especially at Christmas time, especially in the South.
No self-respecting religion can prosper, seems to me
If it starts off with an innocent man, a-hanging on a tree.
Our preachers said if we don't stand, they'll poison everything
And that's what led to the bloody day, the Hangin' of the Greens.
Gary Furr, copyright Gary Furr Music, BMI

The Lord Has Come

The Incarnation was a doctrine I knew nothing about until college and grad school. How could we not talk about it? In this pastoral prayer, given during a series on the Incarnation, I responded to the notion I have in Advent and Christmas that "help has come."

Eternal God, In St. Athanasius's words, you became as we are
      so that we might become as You are.
That journey, so perilous and full of suffering for Jesus,
Undertaken, as the scriptures say,
"for the joy that was set before him."

Happiness comes and goes,
holds us up for a few tantalizing moments,
then drops us again into boredom or anger
depression or anxiety.
We shall have it, we think, by circumstances and
spend our lives working to arrange them just so
or to get to a better one.

Circumstances do not give us joy,
not the joy of Christ that outlasts
wars, hatred, divisions and cancer,
or grief's relentless void.

Christ's joy survived the desert's temptations,
the crowd's constant misunderstandings,
the dark fear of Gethsemane as He knelt to pray,
Peter's denial and Judas' betrayal,
even His disciples' abandonment.
It survived the mocking hatred of the cross itself,
when all turned away and left Him alone to die.

There was joy on the other side of His journey,
joy that Jesus had within Himself but radiated out to all.
It is truly joy to the world,
      joy come into the world,
Joy given to the world,
      joy that overcomes the world,
Joy that saves the world from its pretentious self.
It is the joy that You have given to us
asking only that we love you

>> with our whole selves
>> for the rest of our lives.

It is joy that meets us in eternity,
joy of reunion and recognition and relief.
This is joy that the world cannot take from us.
And so we ask for it, knowing that
it must be given before it can be lived to the last,
and given away before it can be joy everlasting,
In the name of Him who came we do pray, Amen.

This Christmas Eve
Gary Furr, copyright Gary Furr Music, BMI

Writing religious songs and Christmas songs is easy. Writing good ones is the hardest task ever. Writing silly, schmaltzy, corny and lightweight, yes. Worthy to sing again? Not so easy. Anyway, this is my attempt. It's on the "Christmas at Virgin Pines" CD

Band of shepherds in the night,
Without a clue what lay in store.
Heaven and earth brilliant with light,
The hope of something more.

<u>*Chorus 1*</u>
This is the wonder, this is the glory,
This is the mystery,
That a life of flesh and blood came to set us free,
If we can only lift our eyes and see!

Wise men left their homes behind,
Seeking the Truth, with gifts they came,
But you can also journey home
and find it just the same

<u>*Chorus 2*</u>
This is the wonder, this is the glory,
This is the mystery,
That a life of flesh and blood came to set us free,
This the world's desire, this Christmas Eve.

I lift my eyes into the night,
Without a clue what lies in store,
Will I look up and find that light,
the hope of something more?

<u>*Chorus 3*</u>
This is the wonder, this is the glory
This is the mystery--
This my life of flesh and blood, longing to be free
Oh, Divine love, like a sweet dove,
Descend with heaven's peace!
This my deepest prayer this Christmas Eve.

Tentmaker's Hike

Epiphany

Tentmaker's Hike

And what if these seemingly random thoughts,
woven together as "hiking through the wilderness"
tie together more beautifully than even first appears?
That this suffering—and it is—
is not the best thing that ever happened to you,
but the blessings and love and hope amid it truly are.
That the wilderness was the gift given to you,
with its cairns and greenery and peace, long before you needed it.
Love, Eternal Love, anticipates and prepares
like a careful hiker, knowing the grueling trail ahead.
It is the greenhorn, foolish and oblivious,
who assumes it will all work out.

And yet, this seemingly unmarked place
is drenched in invisible markers—
a bending twig here,
a picture of a baby there,
nothing but electrons and waves formed into image,
yet it brings laughter and tears and an ounce of fight.
Poems and prayers and promises and love.
People, intense in their reality and concreteness,
    keep showing up, shaving heads for you,
    even ink on a card or an email in your box offer succor.

This unmarked trail is pretty marked, just not with well-painted signs.
Only fire and cloud and manna in the morning,
    water from the rock,
    and hope from nothing.
Hike on, friend.

Diogenes

I dreamed about Diogenes,
a philosophical man
who wandered ancient Athen's streets
In search of an honest man.

I dreamed he came to America
to start his search anew,
Beginning in the capital
for truth he might pursue

He lost his shirt at knifepoint,
but that did not compare
to the emptiness to come
that left him in despair.

He went to see a spin doctor,
thinking he might help
to sew up all his wounds, but the doctor
turned out to be something else.

It seems this doctor had no skill
except with changing words,
and putting "spins" so bad things
came out good--it was absurd.

He called upon his congressman
who told him not to fret.
Things seemed bad, but they were good,
He shouldn't be upset.

The congressman's opponent,
on the other hand,
Told him things were so far gone
that he'd best leave while he can.

He sent Diogenes to New York,
to change his point of view.
He saw the best psychiatrists, who said,
"Why, the problem is YOU."

"Your mother never loved you,
and neither did your dad.
That's why this robber got your goat
and why it left you sad."

A little of that went a long way,
So Diogenes next tried
To call on Madison Avenue
to seek the truth inside

"Diogy, baby, you're a joke!"
laughed one high-priced exec.
"You've got to change your image, babe
if you want to gain respect"

They made him over sideways,
new clothes, new car, new "do"
He looked as though he owned the world,
but still sought what was True.

Wall Street was his next stop
They suggested that he sell
his lantern and invest the cash
To gain some capi-tell.

"After all," they reasoned,
"You'll need to hire a staff to do
Research if you are ever to find
this truth that you pursue."

And so he wound up destitute
with a case of the desponds,
begging on the New York Streets
for he had invested in junk bonds

He walked out to the Brooklyn Bridge
he was ready just to die
but local news heard about his quest
And put him on at five.

Now he lives in Hollywood,
and does the talk show scene
Promoting his brand new book called,
"Truth is Like a Dream"

And that is when my alarm went off
So I called my boss to say,
"Listen, I'm not feeling well
I'm sure I can't work today."

Living Decisively

Vigilance to one's life is a constant struggle. My inherited limitations and weaknesses drag me into bad habit, but much seems to be a determination to make the world in my own image. I don't want to feel pain, experience reality and face hard truths that cost me something. But I go to church every week to lead others to follow a 1st century Jewish rabbi who told us that we cannot enter the kingdom passively. This was a pastoral prayer about that, although occasion not remembered.

Almighty God,
It is our privilege to live on this side on the Incarnation
and to know the gospel story in the pages of scripture.
We are the heirs of 2,000 years of tradition and practice in Christian history
Most of us have grown up in a Christian culture
and in Christian homes
where the language of the kingdom comes easily to our lips.

With this great privilege comes the awful possibility
that we might not ever access what is so easily available
and live at remove from it as though it didn't exist,
That the freedom of religion we enjoy
might delude us into spiritual malaise
because we no longer live under persecution and crisis.

The great wealth of our knowledge will be useless
if we fail to access its treasures
and live, de facto, in spiritual poverty.
Help us, O God!
Awaken our minds!
Trouble our souls!
Bend our knees,
break our hearts,
breathe Your Spirit into our stubborn wills
that we might glimpse what is ours as inheritance
and take the Kingdom, seize it,
embrace it with all our might. In Jesus' name. Amen.

Calling

I've been called at least once in life
to do one thing,
to do it right.

I have seen with the sharpness of a well-honed knife,
with clarity of heart
and mind.

If but now I could dwell as then within the storms
with fixed intent,
and not react to sharp dissent
or fail to wait when all says, "Quit,"

then I would have moved across a threshold I have prayed about
with all my heart,
to that which exists beyond my wishful states.

I Heard the Trees

I always thought the trees were grasping for the sky,
restrained into resignation by wind, gravity, roots and time,
doomed to fail.
But today I left the city with a solitary mind,
I saw and smelled the earth again for the very first time.
The sky did not mock the earth with indifferent arrogance
as I had always presumed.
Instead, the ground around me thundered silently with life!
A million trees erupted into joy and danced!
A billion blades of grass joined hands and sang!
The roaring upward thrust was everywhere,
as close-containered cars whizzed by
indifferent to the cosmic chorus.
singing in a different key.

But I heard it,
just for a moment!
And I listened
while the sky leaned down to earth to drink it in
and bestow a mother's smile.

More

One day, it struck me that the characters in the Bible didn't pretend to be self-sacrificing as much as we do in our prayers. They were unabashed in asking, begging, demanding from God. Of course, this is true of some of the most tasteless evangelical brands you can imagine, explaining some of our reticence. Still, what if we asked for more instead of less? Still, what to ask?

Almighty God, who gave to us the privilege
by nothing more than fortuitous birth the privilege of living here,
It seems the height of greed to ask for more.
We are supposed to ask far less for ourselves
      and more for others.
But You, the giver of all abundance and life,
      are generous and ready to give to all who ask.
So we implore you to grant us more—
More perspective and patience,
More forgiveness and willingness to forgive,
More peace with the failings of others,
and more acceptance and ownership of our own.
Give us more resignation from blind hatreds, fears and worries,
More trust in You,
More knowledge of the scriptures,
More love for one another and You.
More faith even in uncertainty,
More grace and generosity in privilege,
More spirit of sacrifice and thanksgiving,
More compassionate understanding of our neighbors.
More empathy to the suffering of the weak,
More surrender of our entitlements and pride,
      and more sharing of blessing.
More prayer, more study, more thinking,
More gospel truth and gospel living,
These and more we would ask.
So, give us all You've got!
In Jesus' name. For Jesus' sake. Amen.

A Prayer for Truth

Loving, Amazing, Wondrous, Awesome!
That's You, the God we worship and praise,
Maker of heaven and earth,
Listener to our hearts,
Judge of our lives,
Merciful savior of our souls.
Your love seizes every opportunity to embrace us,
So faithfully that it scares us sometimes.
It is crazy to think we would live our lives
        As though You aren't there,
        that we can do as we please
        or that we can hide some part of us from You.
So lead us to truth in our deepest parts,
        Truth that hurts and then feels better
        Truth that faces facts and accepts them
        Truth that sets us free if we realize we are locked up
        Truth that heals us if we know we're sick
        Truth that reconciles us and returns us home
        Truth that opens the door to endless love. Amen.

Seeking God's Call

A week or so after the Gulf Coast was hit by hurricane Katrina in 2005, a terrible storm that brought death and destruction, and that revealed despair and brokenness in the aftermath, I drove with a small team to assess the damage and what we could do. It was a terrible site to behold—the abandoned cars in the streets of New Orleans, old houses in Gulfport, now ghostly ruins. This was my pastoral prayer after returning. Our church housed refugees who drove all the way to Birmingham to escape the devastation. Churches, volunteers, synagogues and people of no faith, all labels left aside for a moment in the face of human need.

You have called us, Lord
    but not always in the most expected of ways,
        or to the most traveled roads.
We came looking for well-marked highways with plenty of ease,
but found instead a path behind a Savior that leads to Calvary.

Lead us Lord
Even where there is no road at all,
that we might be courageous in walking forward,
Seeking your peace.
We pray for a hurting world today.
In the last few days I have driven from Mobile to New Orleans
And the shores of Pontchartrain and the edge of Gulfport.
What I have seen are people of courage and determination
    but also weariness of soul and spirit
        depression and disarray.

Call us, Lord, as your church in this place,
well-resourced, deeply gifted, able, willing.
to go with you to those people and love them in your name.
Call us, Lord, to the hurting here in our own city who do not know You,
to be unafraid of them or their problems.
Call us, God, to Your work
    in the reconciliation of the world unto Yourself.
What we lack, give us.
For what we face, prepare us.
In what we struggle with inside, heal us,
That your will would be done. In Jesus' name. Amen.

The Bounty of Creation

The church I have served as Pastor since 1993, Vestavia Hills Baptist Church, is a suburban congregation south of the city of Birmingham, Alabama. Our sanctuary sits atop Shades Mountain, a ridge running northeastward along the southern burbs of the city. You can, from the overlook just outside our sanctuary, see the tops of the buildings in downtown Birmingham through the v-shaped cut in Red Mountain to the north where US-31 cuts across it. We have come to see not only the sanctuary, but the natural beauty of our property, as a part of our worship. One side of the sanctuary looks out not through stained glass but simple windows, open to nature, where worshipers can, during a particularly uninteresting sermon or time of deep inner turmoil, look out and see in the distance the view from the mountain. Hawks and wildlife of all kinds meander by sometimes, still living inexplicably in the kudzu and trees, evading the suburbanites as best they can. The Creation, for us, is very close and important. Merely to drive onto our place is to begin worshiping.

Creator God,
As our eyes feast on the colors of spring—the deep-green blooming life,
the brilliant colors of vines and flowers that give us delight
without costing us anything other than our attention--
we are reminded that you are indeed a giver of good and perfect gifts.
What has humankind ever made to match Your wonders?
How can we outdo Your bountiful provision
for our needs and our pleasure?
You have given us not only the elements of survival,
You have given far more—
the richness of family and friends,
the joy of conversation and purpose
and intellectual growth,
Music and art, work and play.

As we remember these gifts and more,
we ask Your help for us
For we are frail and weakened by sin,
so that we take Your gifts
And turn them into problems.
We fail to use them for good
And sometimes turn them to evil ends.

The wonder to us is Your patience with our immaturity
And selfishness and sin.
Forgive us and make us able to rightly enjoy Your gifts.
Liberate us from addiction and idolatry,

That loves them too much.
Deliver us from fear and anxiety
That loves them too little

Free us by Your grace to live as stewards
within the happy bounds of a proper life
that will give us, through wonder, joy and praise
more than we can love with all our might,
through all our days
If only we have the faith and trust to receive them.
In the strong name of Jesus, Amen.

Make Us Instruments of Your Peace

I gave this prayer as a participant in the Mayor's Prayer Breakfast in our community.

God of Peace and all that is right,
Make us who are the objects of Your grace and love
       channels of reconciliation
       proclaimers of good news
       and champions of following Him who taught us peace.

Lord, make us the instruments of Your peace,
real peace.

Where there is hatred, let us sow love,
       but also justice,
       lest we confuse good feelings with right living.
Where there is injury, pardon
       and restitution to the wronged--
       not simply soothing sentimentality
       that prevents our healing with mere catharsis.
Where there is doubt, faith,
       faith born in humility
       free of arrogance and prideful self-congratulation.
Where there is despair, hope,
       not wishful thinking
       or optimistic denial.
Where there is darkness, light,
       and where there is light,
       the willingness to see...
Where there is sadness, joy
       that comes not so much by achieving
       as by yielding
       and loving and giving.

Help us this day,
       on which we have laid aside agendas and phones
       and schedules for this little while
to touch, for these few moments,
deep and quiet places
where our souls are renewed.

Awaken for this hour our
hunger for the things which matter most.

For it is in this moving from the surface to the deep
> that we discover true consolation
> by consoling and understanding,
> by loving and giving,
> by forgiving and dying to self-will and self-serving.

In this journey that we were created to seek,
> which our world so urgently needs
> and from which we too often stray
> we are born to eternal life.

Help us now to truly find that eternal life which is Yours alone to give
> and ours to seek in heart and soul and mind.
> In Your Name we pray. Amen.

Call and Response

Lent

A Prayer for the Beginning of Lent
Based on Psalm 42:8-11

As a Baptist kid in the South, I had never heard of Lent, but I understood "call and response" instinctively. Someone sings and you sing back to them. In southern gospel, it was often something the basses and altos did, little descants under the melody, like a man and woman when they really speak and hear each other's hearts. That's the Lenten journey to me—get quiet, listen and when you finally pick up the song, sing back. You really have to train your ear to hear it.

"By day the LORD commands his steadfast love and at night his song is with me, a prayer to the God of my life. I say to God, my rock, "Why have you forgotten me? Why must I walk about mournfully because the enemy oppresses me?" As with a deadly wound in my body, my adversaries taunt me, while they say to me continually, "Where is your God?" Why are you cast down, O my soul and why are you disquieted within me? Hope in God; for I shall again praise him, my help and my God."   Psalm 42:8-11 NRSV

Shadows fall deep within,
       sometimes never seen but by closest friends,
       and other times, only by me.
Sometimes I know only instinctively,
       by Thee alone.
I do not even know they are there,
I do not know where they come from or why.
Yet other times I know why and cannot bear to see or feel them.

Lift the shadows, send Thy quiet into my heart.
Let me touch Thy holy rest, the untroubled waters of a calm spirit

Today and always,
by the yielding of my broken, sinful, troubled self in trusting love. Amen

He'll Carry You Through
Copyright Gary Furr Music, BMI

I actually wrote the original version of this song in college around 1975, inspired by the songwriting of Kris Kristofferson. Many years later, when I wanted to update it and find a scriptural parallel for it, I was drawn to Psalm 107, which is one of my favorites. It describes four different kinds of trouble people find themselves in. In each case, God rescues them and brings them through.

I was alone in my troubles, I didn't know.
I was lost and uncertain about where to go.
Lost in a wasteland of sadness and sin
until I got on my knees and asked Jesus in.

Chorus
He did it for me--He'll do it for you
Take the Lord's hand, He'll carry you through

You find yourself staring from some prison cell
In chains you created, your own private hell.
Hopeless and broken by the darkness inside,
when suddenly Someone throws the doors open wide!

Chorus
He did it for me--He'll do it for you
Take the Lord's hand, He'll carry you through

>   *Bridge*
>   Sick and forsaken, longing for death,
>   Just wasting away, you labor for breath.
>   What will you do?   Not sure you can stand
>   But that power from nowhere lifts you up again

Out on the ocean of life's stormy sea,
waves of depression were battering me.
I stared at the bottom, afraid I would die,
then there on the waves He came in the night.

Chorus
He did it for me--He'll do it for you
Take the Lord's hand, He'll carry you through

A Song in Our Hearts

This pastoral prayer came at the end of a week when a police officer had been shot and killed. The daily barrage of senseless killings, human violence, war and murder, dulls the senses, but then, when it stops bothering us, who are we? We need to sing and we need to weep. Only God can keep us from being numbed to death.

When we think of how many times in Your Word
we read, "O sing unto the Lord," we realize
that the absence of a song in our hearts is an indicator
of a broken spirit.
For the song in our heart to You,
      is always in response to You
      and an indicator of our awareness of You.
Far too often it is the world's songs that fill our heads
with ourselves and our own lusts.

Sometimes our songs are laments and sad songs
As we sing our pain into the air
and our prayers to You.

But sometimes there is no song at all,
      just the hum of busyness,
      the distracting noise of our own inner voices,
Filled with fears and our pain and our sins
      or the clamor of others' voices
      that lay claim to that which is Yours alone,
and the roar of clashing priorities
from the world around us.

So we know—
There is emptying out to do.
Our minds and hearts need spiritual rest
and cleansing and purging
of those things that pull us from our truest selves
and your kingdom.

For us to pray, "Put Your song in our hearts"
is to ask you to change our lives.
Clean us up, break down partitions,
Sweep away the mess,
Open the doors wide,
That we might let Your song into us.

Fill us with Yourself,
Pushing all pretenders away,
that we might find Your way, which is our way.

We pray this day,
for this world that is filled with
the songs of accusation and blame and greed and sin
      and incomprehensible violence.
We need a song in our hearts for these times.
In Jesus' name.
Amen.

A Prayer for Facing Ourselves

Eternal and Loving God,
We can almost bear Your rejection for our sin more easily than Grace,
For guilt demands a verdict and punishment
And injustice begs to be righted.
Victims' voices fill the universe with tears
and the drums of constant war drown out
any music of the spheres.

Even those without conscience,
who shrink away from responsibility and honor,
neglect duty and follow no calling but self,
Understand the lonely slamming of a locked cell door
and a death sentence for sin.
There is something in us that acknowledges moral truth
even if we will not obey and follow it.

But freely given Grace, is too much to bear.

It is Lent. Everywhere we will ponder heavy disciplines
Powerful practices, resignation and forsaking,
Crosses we will be taking
On our shoulders and around our necks.
Purple is the color of our burden,
Repentance the requirement, confession our lot,
Again and again, we will dwell upon our failings.

Which is why Jesus' invitation surprises us.
Why would You want us, knowing us as You do?
Why keep calling after all these years?
Why will Your love not let us go to our chosen ruin
And suffer our deserved erosion, apathy and neglect?
If You will not tolerate any degree of separation
Why come to us?
We are slammed down by offered forgiveness.
We who shunned reconciliation weep when we meet it.
You turned to us who turned our faces from truth
      and love and beauty and goodness.

Help us in this painful surgery of the soul
To receive grace that does not merely rid us of imperfection
but brings us alive.

Our heart's eye is clouded with grief over our past.
We are dulled by resignation, despair and surrender to what is
So that we forsake the glimmer in our soul of what we might become.

It is grace that grants us the courage to face within ourselves
        what we would most like to avoid

May grace free us to praise you with all our might,
when the burden on our back rolls off us and down
into the tomb underneath the cross.

We have no way to comprehend such love.
Unless you help us.
Let us, as your church, be in the business of healing life
And not merely sustaining it.

If we are too easy on ourselves or unwilling to ask greatness of each other,
Fill us with more faith to believe it.
If we are too comfortable with the status quo,
then rattle us until our eyes shake and our heads spin.
If we are too tolerant of sin and too intolerant of truth,
purge us with the fires of scripture and reality
until we wake up and repent and turn again to life.

If we are lazy and uninterested in the kingdom,
Deliver us from the kingdom of our own smallness.
But above all, may we grasp and be grasped by Marvelous Grace
That lifts our eyes higher so we might glimpse a new possibility.
That we might, in this time of war and hate and anger and rage,
Again not be afraid to hope, to believe, to heal, to bring peace,
To find a way, to make a difference, to live with purpose,
To pray and not give up. In the amazing name of Jesus who invited us along.
Amen.

Being Present

Ever-present Lord,
We confess that we have sinned against you and our own lives
by our failure to live in the present.
Our courage falters and we cave in to anxiety and worry.
We wimp out when we should stand up
    because of fear of what someone might think or say about us
    or our unbalanced need to be liked and approved.
Our desire to love you, obey you and be approved by You alone
    is shoved aside in a moment of forgetfulness.
In pain and hurt, we are swallowed by panic
    that the pain will never end
    and that hurt has no healing.
We are terrified
    and betray our own lips when we said, "I believe in God."
    What good is a faith that never works when we need it most?

Forgive us if we are frightened and forget
that in darkness and light, in joy or tears, You are with us.
When discouragement and resistance are strong,
    our strength sometimes fails.
We take matters into our own hands
and stop listening for the whisper of your Spirit.
We are a hillside withered away by wind and rain;
we feel the erosion of our spirits.

Forgive us that we so easily are distracted from the truth—
In the valley of the shadow, in the presence of our enemies
You are with us.
Our "need" is not for You to be with us. You already are.
We pray that we might be more present to You.
That we would see more clearly
And be rooted and grounded in truth and insight
rather than passing states of mind or external pressures.

In forgiving us, make us whole again, so that we would not simply
see that we have failed, but understand why
And be ready when next we stand the test.
In the strong name of Jesus. Amen.

Weeping With Jesus

I've said all the right things about why Jesus wept
In the thirty fifth verse of the eleventh chapter of John
But He waited a little too long for my taste.
The Bible says he said, "Wait"
The disciples said, "Lord, we better go,"
He said, "No, it isn't time yet."   Too late.

It was poor old Lazarus, who loved Him so.
"Lord, we better go."
But he waited two days "because God would be glorified,"
Jesus said.
Then poor old Lazarus lay dead.

It's a hard, cold truth to get up and go
'Cause you might run out of time
You have some words that need to be said
Before the moment passes by.
History-bound, time-tied, flesh and blood people
Live in chronological jails
Birth, life, work, get old, get sick, then death,
It can't wait—one by one, they go away
The list never grows shorter.

Where did the days go, why didn't I know?
Why did I wait so long?
I see their names,
Lazarus and Charlie and Grandpa and Forrest
Buck and Woody and Wendell and Grace and Grandma,
Sometimes timing was extraordinary sweet

But sometimes it was too late.
Wish I'd been here.
I was on the way
but it was too late.
No anger or hate, but disappointment
that I couldn't be there.
Disappointment with myself.

The list of names grows long with the years,
Conversations un-had,
feelings undeclared.

I weep, but not like Jesus.
I weep for me--
Not the world, or the cross that comes
Just the hell of Death taking one by one
Until they're gone, sixteen brothers and sisters,
Whittling away whole generations out from over me
Then…my turn.

Too late. You had your chance.
Where were you?   If you had been here…what?
It still would happen,
But unlike Jesus, I wept because I WAS too late.
I'm weeping like Jesus,
But is it really too late?
When he said, "Unbind him, let him go,"
What was Jesus thinking, what did he know
That we don't know?

The Journey of Lent

Lent is a time to travel light—stripping away the weight that holds us from running, taking only what is necessary in the wilderness. My people come every Sunday into the sanctuary and I know so many terrible and difficult things they are facing or carrying, yet I have learned that I only know a little of those burdens. It can overwhelm young ministers, this crushing load. We, too, have to learn what must be laid down for only God to carry and what is ours to carry. Lent is a time to remember that again.

God of mercy and might,
Be with us and Your world
as we continue down the path leading to the Cross at the other end,
a place where everything precious dies.
At the Cross
all hope is put to the test, there is only abandonment
and despair and darkness and poison.
We pray for faith that there is indeed something beyond.
For Jesus that something was the cross.
For us, dear God, that "something" might be
the new possibility that lies beyond the failure we fear,
the shame we run from, the excuse we cannot abandon,
the situation we cannot fix, the grief we cannot avoid,
the depression we cannot overcome, the anger we cannot manage.

Beyond these and all others, there is still the possibility
of healing, forgiveness and new life.
We can scarcely believe it
and yet you have put our longing for it in our souls, Lord.
Blow upon the embers of our hearts, so that the flame of love
Might spring to life again where none now is
We pray for the world—
For the poor in body and daily needs
      that they might eat and be strengthened
And for those rich in these things but poor in spirit,
      that they might eat the food which really fulfills.
Be with those who are suffering and be against those who cause suffering
In Jesus' name. Amen.

Cultivating the Lives of Children

Lord God Almighty,
You are the Creator, and in the summer of life,
as in the summers of earth,
You made us for growth and life, both in ourselves and others.
Our children come to us as gift, much like the earth,
Full of life-giving possibility.
Help us to plant in the soil of their souls
the seed that brings forth life—eternal life.

It is given only to You to create seed and bring harvest
We are the workers.
But we pray that we would work faithfully to do what is ours—
To plant Your word in their hearts,
to cultivate it so that they have a chance to grow.

Help us to remove from their way entanglements of our own creation--
The failure to live what we preach,
our own stubborn designs on them instead of Yours
and our own sins and spiritual lethargy
that causes by default damage to those around us
by what we do and by what we fail to do.

Forgive us, we pray, in our stewardship of all our relationships,
for when we could be channels of blessing we are instead
sometimes only hindrances that block the way.
Forgive our contradictions, hypocrisy and weakness.
Purge us of destructive secrets in our lives
and help us as we strive to overcome them.
We pray for the world—that both literally and symbolically poisons the very
Soil and air and water upon which we depend for life.
But also for the poison in the soil of human hearts,
In young minds and memories and histories.
May we be a means of redemption, reclamation and new life
in the midst of a depleted soil,
That love bring an abundant harvest.   In Jesus' name, Amen.

Unraveling

So carefully wound,
tightly pulled and tightly held,
a finger here and there, a thumb if it reaches,
    all so calculated to stay put as long as nothing gives,
    it could even stay this way forever (or so it seemed one time).
    But then the barest thread slips free and
    comes undone and then the whole enterprise comes crashing down
    like invincible paradigms and unsinkable ships
on their maiden voyages,
    moral systems and tightly-clutched beliefs,
    filters on our lives, tenaciously-held,
and reluctantly surrendered
    to the truth about what we feel and what one might do
    given the proper unraveled strings to contemplate.

Then…
  It springs loose and the unraveling begins, so
    dangerous it seems,
but then
    nothing bad happens as
it
should and you are left
    simply unraveled
and that is
all and
while all is not well,
    all is not that bad
        and some
of
  the
dangling
    threads
are
fascinating to the eye
    and lead to deep and previously-unknown spaces in the cave.

Farewell Baby Girl
Copyright Gary Furr Music, BMI

All of my songs are rooted in real experience, not literally, but in the collective experiences I have lived through or read about. Sometimes you "play" with a story rooted in fact. In this case, it was a true event. In South Georgia I was called by my friend the coroner because An infant body had been fished out of the Chattahoochee River, newborn and umbilical cord still attached. He was devastated, as were all the rescue workers on the scene. Why would someone do such a thing to innocent life? We actually had a graveside service for "Baby Jane Doe," and buried her in a donated plot in a sad little area of the cemetery where infants were often laid to rest because their parents could not afford a plot. It was called, mawkishly, "Babyland." TV crews filmed our service and broadcast it, hoping to get information about the child, but none ever came, as far as I knew. That was probably 25 years ago or more, but I have never forgotten her. She is remembered in this song, along with my imagined encounter with the desperate mother in the last verse. "Farther along," said the old gospel song, "We'll understand it." I hope so. I don't understand it now.

I got a call from Billy Joe;
There was something I should know.
The rescue squad had to take
a little body from the lake.
They were daddies, all good men,
the strain of it had done 'em in--
A baby girl, eight pounds or more
still attached to her mother's cord

**Chorus:
So I say, "Farewell, Baby Girl,"
You were all alone in this old world;
Laid down in a borrowed grave,
Where only God can save (you).
We never even knew your name,
Baby Girl.**

We had a service the next day;
It was cold and it was grey.
Whole town came and laid to rest
One who never drew a breath.
They showed it on the evening news
Hoping someone watching knew.
We all watched it in our own homes,
Called each other on the phone and

Said what a shame about

Chorus:
Poor little Baby girl,
You were all alone in this old world,
Laid down in a borrowed grave
Where only God can save (you).
We never even knew your name,
Baby Girl.

Every now and then,
I go to see her grave again.
Sometimes in the cold night air
I see a young girl standing there.
Plastic flowers in her hands,
She just stares and stands.
Sometimes she wipes away her tears,
and runs away when I come near,
and I say

Chorus
Poor little Baby girl,
You're all alone in this old world.
Laid down in a borrowed grave
Where only God can save (you).
And only God knows your name,
Baby Girl.

Beginning Again

God of us all,
our lives lie open before You like a well-worn book,
each sentence, every word, every episode.
There is nothing You do not know about us.

We come to this moment to ask for holy grace;
not to soften the truth of the past
or to blunt the pain of our failures,
but to set them into context.
Only You see our future—for us it is not yet written,
Only You know the mystery of what we will yet be.

We know by the good news of the gospel
that our sins are not the last word about us,
but we struggle to believe this to be true.
The past is so strong, so vivid and real in our memories,
we are hard pressed to put it away from us.

If there cannot be a second place of literal rebirth,
remind us that by the mercy of Christ
there is a place of beginning anew,
where failures are background
for the glory that will be when we at last shall overcome.

Grant us faith to wait on it,
Grant us hope that we would not give up on it,
Grant us love to hold it out to others as well as ourselves.
Through Christ our Lord, Amen.

A Prayer for Justice

Mighty God,
Whose eyes see into our deepest motives
and whose justice is without exception in requirement,
we come as those who have tasted mercy
And now are asked to live it in truth—
People of forgiveness, in the sojourn to wholeness
And learning to live as real neighbors with one another.

Today we listen to what You ask of us all—
To love You truly and with all that we are
and to love our neighbors as ourselves

We need Your help
    To see our neighbors, beyond our own self-preoccupation;
    To hear cries of pain that are sometimes hidden
    by respectability or ignorance or indifference
Make us people who do what is right
beyond what is required and in spite of what we fear.

Give us words to speak for those who cannot speak for themselves
    and deeds to match them,
Hearts that do not collapse in despair at the oceans of need.
Most of all, mold and make us to be like Your blessed Son, Jesus
    To walk as he walked, love as he loved,
be angered at those things that caused him righteous wrath
And welcome those who are excluded
    by systems and selfishness and moral cowardice.
Forgive us for our trembling knees and wobbly faith.
And strengthen us when the tests come as they always do.
Our prayer is that You will be pleased with us in every way
Because we have done Your will from the heart
And done it in deed
And done it in the name of Your love.
Amen.

The Day Alabama Almost Died

All of us who were living in Alabama on April 27, 2011 cannot forget the devastation and destruction as multiple tornadoes, a regular feature of life here, roared across the state and left dozens dead and whole communities razed to the ground. For a long time after, we picked up pieces, came together to rebuild and were reminded again what truly matters.

Video hangs there on the internet,
weathermen almost screaming fear and warning,
Maps lit up with horrible storms, bright, rotating monsters
And the skycam filming it
Dark rumbling cone of cloud, wider and firmer, roaring down,
Swallowing places we all recognized, this street corner, that road,
this hospital and the University itself,
Gobbled into darkness.
We sat watching helplessly in what passes for our safe place,
terrified for people we know and can't call or get to;
Just sat there, watching, listening, praying in a basement or a closet

Now it lives on YouTube and in children's nightmares
Fear comes out of nowhere,
rumbling into a sunny place and wipes it out.
We still remember. How can you forget 63 tornadoes,
taking down a state a town at a time?
Houses blown apart, unglued matchsticks,
flying everywhere. That was the picture everyone shared

But it's the million snapshots, most of them not taken
Sagging shoulders of an old man and his wife
      looking at the wreckage of sixty years.
A family crying over photographs and precious pets and dead neighbors,
Burying the body of a son or a mother or a friend,
Who committed no crime against nature that took their life.
The foolish weakness of our lives pitted against something
      so vast that we shrank away.

Our hearts melted, our schedules crashed,
      our computers went dead with no grid to hook to,
agendas changed, all the foolishness swept away into immediate priority.
Only holding the people we love, finding the body of a lost daughter,
Feeding a neighbor who was hungry and broke,
Losing a job that blew away in a second.
Going to church when it mattered

Listening for God when God seemed gone

Oh, we remember a million snapshots,
of a child calling, "I'm okay," of a house that used to be,
Where a neighbor and his wife died,
their bodies snapped like twigs and tossed into an undignified heap,
Diapers and receipts and toys and furniture,
        curtains and unrecognizable slivers,
trash bags and deck chairs, wood and metal and rope and canvas,
slung in no pattern, no priority and with no respect for their value.
Gone, gone, gone, a house, a town,
        a store where we shopped, a friend we knew.
A way of life we lived, a sense of safety with which we deluded ourselves

But some things still didn't blow away—
faith and hope and love survived,
love for strangers fired up strong and woke us up to one another.
Still, we stood for a moment,
        blown away like the pieces of our lives and our world;
Dazed, disbelief, daunted, discouraged, disheartened, darkened in soul
For just a moment, to take it in.
We will never forget even if we rebuild it all again
What happened that April day.

Hoppers

Some folks change churches more often than they buy a new car or go on a diet. It is a pretty frustrating reality for clergy. We are caught between trying to outperform the competition and grow so someone will think we matter and claiming the high ground from which to hurl disdain and condescension. So you don't have anywhere to express this. I mean, the preachers that rail on against it are, well, preaching at the ones who didn't hop. And, as I thought about it one day, "I'm riled about 'em passing through, but I'd like to be a hopper, too."

How about them church hoppers
Hoppin' them churches?
Toe-stumped, they jump
off'n their perches
They easily whine
with unattended pains
They can't come to see you
Because it might rain.
Hip-hop, belly flop,
Around they go;
Lookin' for a fellowship
Where they can grow.
A preacher that reaches 'em
Tickles and pleases 'em
A man of conviction
who always agrees with 'em.
Where babies never cries
And the food is always good
And the vote always goes
The way they think it should
Where they outlaw Halloween,
and poor Santa Clause
And hop on the van to
Promote their latest cause.
How 'bout them church hoppers,
wallets snappin' shut ,
Explainin' that they love you
in Jesus, brother, BUT...
How 'bout them church hoppers?
hoppin' them churches
Standin' on convictions
to leap from their perches
How 'bout them church hoppers?

A Prayer to Be Still

These minds of ours are too busy.
They are little children clamoring for our attention.
Even when it is time to give it to you,
things to be done, worries, fears, random thoughts.

Be still and know, be still so we CAN know.
When we ask for stillness,
      it is not a plea for escape from daily responsibility.
It is not so that we may somehow be happy all day
In a world of suffering such is unreasonable and unspiritual

The peace we ask for is your peace—not the peace that escapes
      or that buffers or is a tranquilizer to the soul.
It is the piercing silence that clarifies,
      shows us our sins and faults that we may find grace.
It is the terrifying silence of solitude that
      brings us before Your holiness
      with nothing but hope in our hands.

Clarksville, Tennessee in 1963

In 1963 I was in Clarksville, Tennessee
Daddy had just moved us there with his company.
I didn't know the South was not the entire world
My cousin had a beach towel with a squinting rebel who said said,
"Forget HELL!" I didn't know what it meant
My great grandfather took a rebel stand
And at 42 took up arms against the Yankees, whose team in New York
I rooted for, without seeing the irony.
He fought for the hopeless cause and the dark night.
I didn't know. How could I?
A child doesn't know what a shadow is
      until someone tells them.
"Why, you make it yourself, when you block out the light."
A baby just toddling stares down
at the shadow walking with him on the ground.

When I lived in Clarksville, Tennessee we went
      to a big Baptist church whose pastor sent
      every child a birthday card, we learned music and rules
and learned about Jesus in Sunday School.
"Deep and wide," we would sing
and "Jesus wants me for a sunbeam,"
and "Jesus loves me this I know,"
For the Bible tells me so."
"Jesus loves the little children,
All the children of the world,
Red and yellow black and white,
They are precious in his sight,
Jesus loves the little children of the world."
When the time was right, we would give our heart
To Jesus and be baptized to get a new start.
We gave money to send missionaries
who told foreign people about our loving God.
We all had our own churches for both races,
Same Jesus, same Bible, but in separate places.

So from North Carolina to Clarksville, Tennessee in 1963
      where picnicking families like us came to see
      soldiers from the 101st jump out of planes,
      Float down out of the sky on Sunday afternoons.
My school was only children who looked and talked like me,

Soft southern accents and watching TV,
Where all the people looked like us,
Jed and Granny and Andy Griffith and Mr. Green Jeans.

Don was a black man who worked for Daddy.
He swept the floors
and kept the stockroom clean.
He loved my Dad, who treated him like a man.
When we moved later Don wanted to come,
this time above the Mason-Dixon line,
but the company said no and he went back to Tennessee,
To Clarksville, in 1963.

In Clarksville, Tennessee in 1963
In the little neighborhood, where my brothers and me
Would go outside all day, until Mom yelled outside
To come to supper. Unsupervised, we rode our bikes
Behind the mosquito truck, pretending to be fighter planes
in the toxic clouds.
We had no idea you could die from DDT
or that everyone else in our world wasn't white like me.
It was safe and beautiful, or seemed to be.
South of where we lived a man stood in a doorway and
Swore something called segregation would always be.
Some troops with rifles came
And those children went to school anyway,
But the man who swore never said, "I'm sorry."
Like my mother made me do
when I hit Julie in the nose with a dirt clod and she told on me.

A helicopter crashed in Viet Nam that year
The jumpers on Sundays would be dying there soon.
A man named Bull Connor turned dogs loose on children
Down in a city called Birmingham in May,
    while my brothers and I innocently played
       and where I would make my home one day.
We calmly rode our bikes unchaperoned to school a mile away

Then in September somebody bombed a church.
Four little girls died in a Sunday School room.
They were praying just like we were taught to do.
They died in God's sanctuary on Sunday morning.
It came with no warning.

A stick of dynamite blew out the stained-glass Jesus' face
And hate boiled over about something called race.
We watched on our black and white TVs
The girls were not much older than me.
Everyone worried. We were afraid,
but Dad opened the store as usual next day.
People bought bobby pins and underwear and candy by the pound
And 45 rpms with Elvis' new sounds
The changes were still far away from us and me
In Clarksville, Tennessee in 1963.

The Cross through the Window

Holy Week

The Cross through the Window
Copyright Gary Furr Music 2004
From the album "permanent world of ṭ

For me song ideas, poems, even sermons and prayers just rise up out of listening, watching, absorbing what is going on where I am. Since I am in a car on the way to do religious things a lot (ominous shadows from the Good Samaritan pop into mind) I see a lot of life around me. You look into the next vehicle. One day, I stopped at a light and next to me was a van full of very tough looking guys, maybe headed for work, or back to the shelter, couldn't tell. I felt a flash of judgment shoot across my consciousness and then in the same split second, all the way through their van, I saw a church and a cross on the building lined up perfectly next to the face of the driver and then shame of recognition. And then an idea for a song.

I was sitting at an intersection at the end of the day;
A dirty van pulled up beside me, three or four men, hard to say,
I judged them to be trouble, poor and not my kind,
Then my eye looked through the window all the way, to the other side
And I saw a sign and I saw a sign.
There was a cross on a church, it was thick and deep and strong,
I saw it through their window saying, "Something's wrong!"
Reminder of a story that once had saved my life,
All at once I was ashamed. It cut me like a knife.
And I wondered if I'd failed to see the men that they could really be
When I saw that cross through the window.

I was walking with my head down in a hospital hall,
A lot of people in trouble, they were sitting near the wall.
I stood and looked outside just to catch the view
Above the heads of fellow sufferers waiting on bad news
and I saw a sign, and I saw a sign.
There was a cross in a graveyard on a distant hill nearby,
I saw it through the window as it caught my eye.
I thought how out of place it looked in this nice part of town
where all the people look good and they never fall down.
But I wondered if I'd understood all the things about them that I should
after I saw that cross through the window.

You can hang a cross around your neck or stick it on your car,
but it won't do you any good 'til it tells you who you are.
Some are outside the gate, some are markers by the road,
a cross where somebody died, it can be a heavy load.
The love we say we're looking for in the name of being free
has a costly love to show us if only we will see
the cross through the window that cross through the window.

The Minister (1992)

He stands, gaunt and gentle in his well-fitting suit;
Wire-rims circle his soft eyes without contrast--
The effect is intensely ordinary.
He always wears a seatbelt, exercises sanely.
Eats balanced meals whenever he can
(Having seen the fruit of excess at the bedside every day).

No yeller or screamer, he; always good in a meeting,
able to tell a joke (clean or corny only, please).
His body is restrained, neatly-dressed, every hair in place,
buttons down, after shave ever so lightly-applied;
(enough for scent but not attraction to all those lonely women).
He is tense and calculated at the same time,
a posture chosen to offend no one, affirm everyone,
and soothe the savage beast.

He dispenses grace in measured doses
A marriage here, a grief there, it drips
and runs and spreads a paper-thin layer
across the multitude of heartaches that forcibly
assault his heart each day.
His voice is thick and velvet-soft, almost slushy
      with well-rehearsed winsomeness.
The words are rarely crisp, never harsh--
except when preaching against some non-existent demon
      to the demon-possessed.
No real truth is ever uttered without first adjusting it
      to comfort and soothe.

He's the resolution of his mother's sorrow;
      the fulfillment of her dreams,
         serving a distant Father,
The Pieta without the cross
      from which to lower his already broken body
But Mary's tears now are for a lifeless form that died long before it could be lifted to a cross that matters.

No blood.
No holes.
No thorns.
No spitting mockers.

Only deadness.
Death
of mind and spirit,
in flesh and loin,
 within the heart.
He would gladly be nailed to something
         if he could only find someone with a hammer,
For no one makes crosses anymore--they just
ride in cars, sit at desks, talk on phones
arrange meetings and work at win-win situations.
People come and sit and listen
         and then do it anyway.

He's thought about his Myers-Briggs;
therapeuted until his soul was drained.
He pays the bills, buries the dead
and lives to near, "Nice sermon, Rev."

Somewhere in his secret place
a wicked passion lives
To yell an expletive or two
         and run away
                 without luggage or plan
to look for God again
instead of women in church
or churchless men.

Lose control and dance and weep,
Risk his life,
         laugh unconstrained;
Lie down in uninhibited sleep.
Throw away a good career
to follow an intuitive tear
across the world or into the dark.
Make a choice that isn't clear;
Quit a job.

Not today, though.
Maybe someday,
         maybe even tomorrow.
But the people are here;
something has to be said.

He breaks the bread and blesses the cup
raises it up
and sips, not drinks
the bloody sup.
a memorial to a Man who, unlike he
only got to eat it once;
but by God once was quite enough.

The Solid Rock

Almighty God
You are our solid rock, our firm foundation.
Winds of change come and blow through our lives.
Sometimes the wind is gentle and we sway and bend
       and the wind passes and all is well.
But there come times when raging windstorms rage,
       and everything familiar is stripped away
One by one our props and comforts and supports blow out of sight
       and we are hanging by a thread.
If we turn our eyes from Jesus,
       from the hope we know,
       from the faith we received,
we are blown by every confusing wind that swirls around us—
other people's opinions and a changing world,
the ravages of time and aging,
our own shifting mental states.

If nothing else remains the same but You, Lord,
help us to keep our eyes fixed on you.
so that we may always know where we are.
Send us where we need to go.
Let our hands fasten to your word,
which is a firm and steady rock in confusing times.
May our hearts rest on our hope in you.
May our actions and attitudes be formed and shaped
       only by modeling our lives after Jesus
and building houses on firm foundation that cannot shake. Amen.

That Kind of Love

Theories of atonement are important the same way guard-rails are. They can help you not drive off a cliff but they can't take you home. The story of Holy Week is a story to be lived into, walked with, experienced from within. My fellow songwriter Pierce Pettis wrote a beautiful song called, "That Kind of Love" and says "Everything will fall in time, except those things that cannot die, that kind of love, Oh, may you be remembered by that kind of love."

Amazing, Astounding, Loving God,
Incarnated in Jesus Christ,
Who loved the disciples when they overestimated themselves,
gave to them a loyalty they could not keep in return,
loved the crowds who turned on a dime against Jesus--
Jesus, who loved the Pharisees and scribes and leaders
  even as they plotted to kill him
  and the Romans who carried it out
  and the disciples who forsook him when they did,
Jesus who so loved your enemies who have persecuted the church
  Attacked its truths
  Rejected its claims
  Opposed your kingdom
  And ignored your call and claims;

God who so loved the world that continues to resist,
  confident it can do everything in its own might,
  by ignoring the one who gives all strength to do all things,
If you so loved them and us and the world
that you gave your only Son,
Maybe You can love us, now, too
  in our most unlovable and broken places
  in the sin we hold onto
  in the grief we cannot bear
  in the call we will not answer
  in the pain we won't let go.
  In the grievance we are yet to forgive
In such a week as Holy Week,
that moved from waving palms to hammered nails,
You still so loved the world and us, and gave your only Son
  for us and for all.
That kind of love calls us to renewed faith and replenished hope
And resurrected, forgiving love. Amen.

Handel's Messiah

Handel's Messiah belongs now to the world, but it is performed and associated by many with Advent and Christmas. The first performance, however, was in Dublin during Eastertide. This is the challenge of telling the Jesus story. Wherever you start, you must eventually tell the rest of it. This great choral work is not unlike the Christian kerygma in the sermons in the book of Acts—they tend to tell the story compactly, but connected from Israel to the end of time and the middle of time, the center, being the birth, life, death and resurrection of Jesus. The past leads to it, the future comes from it.

Invocation

Loving God,
We long for the psalmist's assurance that
"light dawns for the righteous,
and joy for the upright in heart."
In this world so full of heartache and crushed hopes,
We need a beautiful song again--
The vision of glory,
The ministry of true reconciliation,
The confidence of faith,
The healing power of love,
and the sustaining energy of biblical hope.

We pray for joy, O Lord.
Today we come to hear the gifts of these musicians,
Who offer to enlarge our hearts and minds through glorious sounds.
May they be vessels of your Spirit today
and their gifts multiplied in our hearing.
We have come, too, to offer ourselves in worship,
to give our time and attention to the things of the kingdom and
by our listening, our giving, our fellowship and our love.

Please receive all these gifts—our faithful offerings and tithes,
our time, our music, our attention, our love,
as a small and humble way to say, "We love you, Lord."
Today we remember Jesus, the Christ, come in the flesh
To teach us how to die—and how to live. Amen.

Benediction

We beheld his glory, full of grace and truth.
Our minds and eyes and ears are full of this truth today.
Our hearts are satisfied. We feel God's peace.
Can we do any better than to welcome one another
        into his kingdom
           and the journey of discipleship?
Let us go with joy today and to the work that really matters. Amen.

Christ the Song

A seminary classmate said that his grandfather in East Tennessee has a stock prayer for every occasion in which he intoned, "Bless those whom it is our duty to pray for," as a sort of catch-all. We preachers can fall into that as well. I have taken it as a challenge to always try to speak a fresh word that fits the moment. There is a worship of "spontaneous" in my tradition that tends to turn into "monotonous." It is no virtue to always shoot from the hip, especially when it is the same hip over and over. This was a prayer offered before a choral program. I always seek to write such prayers from the heart, laboring over my words. If they do not turn out well, it is not for lack of thinking carefully about them. And I never reproach sermons in prayers—I'm not preaching. I' trying to speak for my people and for me.

Eternal God,
We have come here, now, to this moment and to this place
to listen and to receive;
To comprehend yet again the great song of salvation
found in the story of Jesus
whose birth was an announcement of hope to sinners,
whose life and teachings brought life into richest harmony,
whose courage was like the sound of a friend's voice in the night.
He died on a lonely cross
as we heard the awful requiem of humanity's own righteousness
and then would come the grace note of Easter morning,
the song that set us free indeed.

We are here to listen, to receive, to give thanks, to pray, to praise
and glorify you, the one true God,
for the countless variations on the one theme—
Christ in us, the hope of glory.
Amen.

Words Fail
Copyright 2003, Gary Furr Music BMI

This is probably just me, but I find writing songs about my faith to be incredibly difficult. Maybe it's my fear of triteness, of making something so important to be glib and breezy. It's easy to fall into musically boring and theologically uninteresting telling of the greatest story ever told and retold and retold. That's the problem. It's been done really well. How to make it heard as though for the first time? I gave it a try and this resulted. A song, ironically, about how hard it is to find words. Still, at a few moments in my life, God's reality has felt this way to me. I am speechless. So I wrote about that.

Chorus
Words fail to say I love you
It's too tender for a crowd,
Even saying them out loud
Words fail, Words fail.

The ways you stood by me, never denied me
To know you still believed in me
I start to sing your praise and tears roll down my face
Streams of love so deep and strong
That words seem wrong

Chorus

I've read the Book and sung, of the victory He won
Seen the mystery that hung
upon a savage cross, where hope seemed to be lost
Instead of death we found Easter from the ground

Chorus

Bridge
I feel it when I wake up
and in the day I take up what I gave up in the night
When everything seems lost, I remember what it cost
Everlasting Love rains down from above

So when I bow my head to pray
and somehow fail to say it and my words are not the best
You look beyond the surface and all the worst inside us
To see the heart within where holy songs begin

Chorus

Forgiveness
Copyright Gary Furr Music BMI

This is a song that emerged out of a collection of memories, thinking and preaching. A few real stories from my ministry, pain I've listened to, pain I've read about, pain I've lived myself. Forgiveness is the whole thing—either we get it or miss Jesus altogether. He came, taught us about it, showed us how to announce it and live it, then died with it on his lips. It's amazing to me still that it happens.

Don't even have to pull a trigger--
Words do the trick just as well.
The damage accumulates in bits and pieces
    and love crumbles into hell
        with arguments to justify yourself
        and truth a weapon in the way we tell.

<u>Chorus:</u>
It's impossible to give forgiveness.
It's even worse to have to ask.
If letting go is the answer,
Living like it's gone is the task.
How else you going to deal with the past?

How do you tell the mother of a victim
That it's time to let go and embrace?
She closes her eyes at night to be haunted
by the anger and the emptiness and waste
and requests to grant the killer grace
and the image of her son's smiling face.

<u>*Chorus:*</u>
It's impossible to give forgiveness.
It's even worse to have to ask.
If letting go is the answer,
Living like it's gone is the task.
How else you going to deal with the past?

    Bridge:
    Deep inside I knew it would hurt her
    the moment I inflicted the wound,
    But pride and stubbornness turned into years
    Though I promised I would fix it soon.

It's a miracle to be forgiven.
Even more when we don't have to ask.
If dying on a cross is really dying for us all,
Then love is something you don't have to grasp,
Grace is a lifeline that Someone else cast
And forgiveness is a gift and all you do is pass it
To someone else who's sinking fast.

<u>*Chorus:*</u> **(tag repeat)**
It's impossible to give forgiveness.
It's even worse to have to ask.
If letting go is the answer,
Living like it's gone is the task.
How else you going to deal with the past?
How else you going to deal with the past?

Michael
Copyright Gary Furr Music, BMI

I write about my experiences in ministry and that means I write a lot about human suffering. This song is an early one, from college days in the 1970s. It wasn't my experience, but a friend's cousin, a young man diagnosed with cancer. It was one of my early encounters with the relentlessness of death and dying in the world. The last verse was added just in the last dozen years, as I thought about the oddity that while the great drama of dying goes on every day, now gathered up in hospitals where the healthy don't have to see it and the rest of us go on with our business...

Michael found out that he's dying.
They gave him a month or two to live.
For the first time in his young life,
Some of the pieces didn't fit.
"Oh, my God," he cried, "After I have died, will there have been a reason?

He kissed his wife and held her close.
As she wept she spoke her pain out loud.
 "Why did this happen to me?
I'm just a face in the crowd.
Alone that night she cried, "After Michael dies, will I have a reason to live?"

Days of treatments while they prayed.
Michael rarely left his room.
One night he told her, "I am afraid
that when the time comes I won't know what to do.
I want to be so strong, but I hope it won't be long until I see the light of day.

In the restaurant down the street
Friends were laughing off the day.
The night was young, their work complete
Now they could drink their stress away.
While they raised a toast to what mattered most
     in a room nearby someone prayed
        for one who'd finished his last day,
Closed his eyes and slipped away.

The Power of Surrender

Lord, if we might ask one thing and only one,
What would it be?
Our problem is not always merely commitment of the will;
      it is also attention to what matters.
Our choices are so many they overwhelm us
Our lives are so busy and full
that we suffer from sensory overload, not deprivation.
It is not merely choosing the right that challenges us
      but the spiritual calm within to make a good choice.
We are affected by all around us--
      The people in our lives
      The pressures we live under
      The past we drag around with us
      The noisy voices in our heads
           of what others think we should do.
The million clamoring sounds of our culture
claiming our time and attention and energy.
Responsibilities that weigh on us.

We can go away, but these all go with us.
So we ask this day for the power of surrender
To release us from the need to control all of life
Fix every problem, overcome every failing,
Heal every relationship we've hurt, achieve every goal,
Meet every need, live up to every expectation.

Instead we ask for the grace to turn loose and let go
And make room for your provisions in our inner lives
Open space for your priorities,
For peace and stillness to replace the noise
And grace to wash over us like cool rushing waters
On a hot summer day,
Refreshing, quenching and replenishing us.
For we live amid times of death, destruction and decay
And we need to know the one true thing more than ever.

What It Is
Copyright Gary Furr Music BMI

This was the title cut on my third CD and it's about…well, you know what it is.

It's a wildfire burning--
Two bodies craving
A stone of stumbling, the give you're taking
It'll lay you low on a mountaintop
it turns you loose and you can't stop
that's what it is.

It's a twist of fate, change your life
Makes a man take a wife
It can wreck your plans, it's blinded rage
It's the safest place, make you afraid
That's what it is.

Chorus:
That's what it is, that's what it is,
That's what it is

It's buried treasure.
It's the chance you lose.
The lifeline that you're holding to
A mother's touch, a baby's hand
Keeps a daddy coming home again,
That's what it is.

Chorus:
That's what it is, that's what it is,
That's what it is

It's naked touch when you've been apart
It's a second chance for broken hearts
Sweet memories you thought were lost
It can make your day,
It can hang a cross--
That's what it is.

Chorus:
That's what it is, that's what it is,
That's what it is

Rutter Requiem

Thanks to being in a church with a world-class musician and choral director, Dr. Terre Johnson, and our incredible choir, I have been able to hear and learn about some of the great music of the Christian church. I gave this following a presentation of the Requiem by John Rutter, a beautiful and somber remembrance of human sorrow. Before we can hope again, we must grieve honestly to reckon our loss.

We came here tonight to wait and to hope
That tombs and sorrow and death and loss
Are only prelude
To seek the Living shepherd,
Beyond our doubts, beyond our fears,
From death into life.
We wait faithfully
Hoping that
You might meet us in our gardens of sorrow as you met Mary,
We wait for unexpected visions in the midst of our tears.
And for you to come to us
As you came to them behind the locked doors of fear
To wait tonight is enough
For tomorrow we will walk to the tomb again
And discover the promise fulfilled yet once more
Tonight it is enough to shed out tears and grieve
For joy comes in the morning
And there is a purpose to the night that cannot
And should not be passed by
For when the morning comes
Its light is ever more brilliant
And our joy everlasting.
We wait as the people of faith. In Jesus' name. Amen.

In-between

I'm looking around for it
when the warehouse is about to close and
everyone but one other guy and I are gone
and we're just sweeping the floors
before they close her up.

When the lights go out and the stores shut down
and the mall is dark
except for the pallid illuminations of a few stubborn bulbs,
All else is inhaled into night.

When the theme park closes and nothing moves
I'm always looking
behind the facades put up
by clever theme park designers
and computer animators
Who deceive us into make-believe futures
And distant pasts.
But the spell breaks. I see exit signs and emergency stairs
and evidence of the workers.

Graduation is done, the candidates and their families
Have snapped enough photos to post
Ephemeral proof they were here and did something
And were somebody.
The cars have all left the parking lot
Classrooms empty.
The floors will be stripped and waxed next week
The staff is tired and it's time to go
It is a cavern, dark and empty and lifeless.

I search heaven and earth for the something that is there
after the bright lights blink out with a single switch
and all the sly devices stop their whirring deceptions,
what is this thickness, unbearable stillness,
the absence of anything, but
in the silence, says my heart, there must be something,
there must be.

Running From the Tomb

Easter

⁸ So they went out and fled from the tomb, for terror and amazement had seized them; and they said nothing to anyone, for they were afraid—Mark 16:8

Easter

Lord of Life
    On this most holy day, we sing with all our hearts,
        for we have gone to the tomb and it is empty.
What did we expect?
    The same everyday dreary death and darkness
        that pervades our lives?
    The same monotonous routines?
    The same unchanging fates?
    The same sad arrangements of who is up and who is down
        and who isn't counted?
The same sad aching griefs of loved ones gone down into the earth?
The same impending void of sickness and death?
    We have no vision of life, only the weariness of sin.

We went to the graveyard to tend it and shed some tears
    and found instead an angel and Your holy, shocking word
    "He is not here, but is risen, as he said!"

O glorious Jesus, risen Christ,
    fill us with laughter to swallow up our tears
    lift us above the darkling plane of this world to see
        the horizon of hope ahead--
        Our tragedies transformed,
            our memories safeguarded,
                our love secure,
                      our salvation done.

Jesus Christ, glorious Lord, blessed brother, deepest friend
    we love you; we cry out at the sight
        of the empty tomb that filled us with faith
            and chased away the spiritual night.

God, who so loved the world, who so loves us,
    our paltry faith is now revived as Christ was raised
        raised to walk again in the Spirit you so gladly give.

Today our sins shrink into insignificance
    evil is dealt a fatal blow.
No self-proclaimed evil kingdom can stand
    the saints gone on before laugh and sing in heaven
    if only we could see!

Mighty God who raised the Son in power
        raise us up with Him,
To renewed life and faithfulness
        grant us eyes to see what our imaginations
        could not create
Send us, then, running from the grave with a shout,
        For you are alive and everything is made new!
Halleluia! Amen!

Resurrection

O God
We call you by many names:
Creator, Savior, Holy Spirit,
Friend, Judge, Truth, Love and you surpass them all

But today you are the Surprising God
Who turned the darkness of Maundy Thursday
      into the light of Easter morn,
Broken hopes into new possibilities,
Deniers into apostles,
Cowards into martyrs,
A ragtag band into a church,
Murderous Enemies into brothers and sisters,
A dying thief into a man of faith,
a pagan world into a Christian culture,
marginal people into those called and elect,
despised sinners into disciples.

Everything changes because of You
Who did not have to do it, did not have to love us,
Did not need us or have to involve yourself with us,
Except that you are love itself!
Our hearts are full of happiness and joy today
Because of Your Surprising power to change the game.

The world is full of pain and war and the stupidity
      Of the human race
      Hunger, hurt and sadness.
But this is a day for energy and hope,
Inspiration and aspiration,
Ecstasy and euphoria,
Dancing and shouting,
Laughter and praise.
How could we know?   Who could imagine?
What a God!   How can we fail to hope again,
      If you are capable of turning worlds upside down,
      Lives inside out,
      Darkness into light,
What might you do with me?   With us?

Sky's a-Clearing
Copyright Gary Furr Music, BMI

When I set out to sing about grace, it came out as this song. Once I read a sermon that asked the question, "Does the resurrection happen?" This song was about Easter happening when you had despaired that it could. I love this song. It is my hymn of grace. I am a witness. Resurrection happens. Every day.

Had my head down for a long time
Same thoughts running 'round in my weary mind
Dead-end road and a heavy load
Weighing down on me
Then one morning without warning
I was free

All the preaching that I listened to
Told me bad news was always fixing to
Come crashing down like an avalanche on my worthless soul
But love surprised me as far as the eye could see
Everything was whole

Chorus
**Sky's a-clearing, the time is nearing
The clouds are breaking up,
     my hopes are waking up
he burden's lifting, life is shifting
     And I have the strength to go on**

I've been counting all my blessings
Finding grace after confessing
All those hands that I once slapped away
Still reaching out to me
And now I hold on like a drowning man in an angry sea.

Chorus

On the one hand, I'm less certain
Of what might be behind the curtain
The easy answers, like a cancer
Leave you looking for a friend
But on the other, I've discovered
A Love that never ends

Chorus

Beginning Again

God of us all
Our lives lie open before you like a well-worn book.
Each sentence, every word, every episode,
There is nothing you do not know about us.

We come to this moment to ask for holy grace,
Not to soften the truth of the past
Or to blunt the pain of our failures,
but to set them into context.
Only you see our future—for us it is not yet written
        Only you know the mystery of what we will yet be.

We know by the good news of the gospel
        that it is not the last word about us.
But we struggle to believe this to be true
        The past is so strong, so vivid and real in our memories
We are hard pressed to put it away from us.

Remind us that by the mercy of Christ
There is a place of beginning anew,
Where our failures are taken into us as background
For the glory that will be when we at last shall overcome

Grant us faith to wait on it,
        Grant us hope that we would not give up on it
Grant us love to hold it out to others as well as ourselves.
        Through Christ our Lord, Amen.

"Awakening"

Reflection on the Music by Rolf Lovland

Gary Allison Furr

"Awake."
A voice? Deep within. Where did it come from?
"Lazarus, come forth."
Long ago. But just now. I am wrapped in strips of death
    My heart sodden with other people's resignation and despair for me.
    I long quit living. I still exist. But not alive.
    Who said that? Where did it come from?
"Come alive. Beloved. I have called your name."
    Who are you? And why would you call me? Here? Now?
    Just when I had adjusted to subsistence of the heart
    To scraps from life's table.
    I had resigned myself to this dark cave where the light is barely enough.
    Why hope now?
"Because. The world needs people who have come alive. You need to live before you die. You need to know the glory that is you. The power of love in your flesh and mind,
A heart alive, aflame with newness. Because I love you."
    I only feel the tears that sting my eyes
    I cannot think. What on earth is this love that surges in us?
    I cannot believe it so. It fits nothing I have. I am not trained, I don't see how…
"Just be still and take the gift. Open it. Cherish it. Receive it into yourself. Do not question or complain or become anxious. See it through. Stay true. Be yourselves."
    But Love, how? How?
"Time enough for that. Just embrace this gift. Accept my love, open your arms and do not shut out all the other love that is yours because you are accustomed to deprivation.
There is room for all Loves. Cherish. Embrace. Love. Hold them close."
    "But…"
"Get up, you have been a child long enough. Now you are a man. Take hold and love."
Come on. Love awaits."

It is morning. I walk in the darkness, music in my ears and a flame in my chest
    My steps are quick, my breathing close, my heart alive with You.
    Love.

People of the Resurrection

O Lord, in the brilliant light of the resurrection,
> every sin is exposed to the light of love and all
> darkness banished by grace.

Every doubt is vanquished and every denial turned to true obedience.
In the day of the resurrection we see love demonstrated on a cross
> justice vindicated against injustice

We now know that if anyone is in Christ, there is a new
creation.
We may yield our stubborn wills before the truth and be set free.
We are liberated to forgive the hurts done to us by others
We confess that we are sinners, not in order to live in shame,
> but to declare that all might be released from its
> power and filled with new life.

Help us to live as resurrection people, now and always, through Jesus
Christ our Lord, Amen.

I Missed the 1960's
Copyright, Gary Furr Music, BMI

This relatively new lyric came about one day as I was pondering over the 1960's and all the changes that happened and how, as a child and later as an adult, I was mostly a viewer. I meet these people who went to Woodstock and Selma and the March on Washington, but most of us simply went to school, went to work, went home at the end of the day and were spectators. That is almost always the way it is with change. Still, we are changed anyway—whether we supported it, fought it, or just watched it on the news. Question is, what are we sitting back and watching now? Time to rise.

I missed the 1960's, people trying to be free
I was just a kid in school, so I watched it on TV.
Crowds of people marching, others dropping out
World of changes headed for my homeland in the South.
Coming up around the bend, way too quick to see
I missed the 1960's, but they didn't miss me

I didn't go to Woodstock, but I listened to the sound
Didn't do the drugs that saturated my home town
I went to church and kept the rules, didn't do my thing.
But I listened to the Beatles, Bobby Dylan, & the King
the walls on which the prophets wrote
      were cracking at the seams.
I missed the 1960's, but they didn't miss me.

Never worked for NASA,
      but I saw Neil Armstrong land
And end the race to outer space
      with a giant leap for man
I didn't march at Selma or go hear Dr. King
But the world my Daddy worked for
      was fading like a dream.

I watched the news of wounded boys
      on stretchers under fire
Knew a kid with long hair who'd call the government liars
He was at Kent State the day the guardsmen lost their cool
And blood from Vietnam spilled in the middle of that school
When Nixon finally called it quits I was number Fifty Three
I missed the 1960's but they didn't miss me.

Sexual revolution, a generation gap
Freedom and tradition in a perfect storm of facts
Women soon stopped asking for permission for a life
You could marry and have babies,
      but you didn't own your wife.

People started saying that the earth was running out
Acid in the air and famine coming after drought
Nuclear Armageddon, politicians on the fence,
The Book of Revelation said we'd better all repent.
Hal Lindsey said the world would end around 1983
I missed the 1960's, but they didn't miss me.

It's hard to see the highway when you're riding in the back
Looking for somebody to help get your life on track
If I'd known that I was living in such crucial times
I'd have paid better attention, maybe gotten out of line.

Then I was too busy; Now, I'm sixty years of age
I tell myself it's time for someone else to be up on the stage.
These times, they are a changin', too, changing mighty fast
I offer up excuses for living in the past.
But sometimes voices come, calling from my memory,
I missed the 1960's, but they didn't miss me.

A Blessing for Second Times

The wonder of newness, first tries, first love appears
        And never again is felt as novelty.
In delicious delight the unknown is uncovered
Thereafter only lost and found, but never again discovered
The yearning for infancy and helplessness and newness
        perplexes us once we have seen ripening, and maturity
        development, and gritty perseverance.
But redemption begins with a need to find anew, be
Transformed, recreated, restored, reborn.

After a skinned knee, walking wobbly toddlers
Bicycling children, and soggy skiers
Get up to try again, and maybe this time
There is a different sweetness, found in the getting up,
        in love lost, grief borne, life learned,
That makes the seconds special in their own way
To have loved and lost is better I suppose,
Than never to have loved,
But what of those who have loved and lost
And find courage to love again?

I tell you, there is something extraordinary
        In the getting up and getting on
        The holding up and holding on
To let yourself go again to a place
        Now knowing what it holds, how it is,
        And that it will be its own true place,
Going there is special and sacred, too.

So here's to second times around, second loves,
        Second tries, second hopes, and even second thoughts,
For the courage and joy, this time fully wise and true,
        fully known and fully given, and eyes wide open.
There is something really special about that, too.

Welcome to Regrets
Gary Allison Furr, Pat Terry and Katie Furr
Gary Furr Music/BMI all rights reserved

"Welcome to Regrets" is a song that I wrote in 2014 with the great songwriter Pat Terry and my daughter Katie Furr, who gave me the original idea. One day she said, "Dad, I have an idea for a song—a tattoo parlor in Brooklyn where old hipsters can go to get their tattoos removed." Great idea! So I set out to write it. Originally, I went for funny and wrote all the "droopy tattoo" ideas you can imagine. When I pitched this to Pat when we were together for him to lead a workshop, he suggested it had some rich possibilities for a serious story song. I liked that. I prefer going for the non-obvious. But I was stuck after setting it up to find an ending. Then I heard a real story that made the last verse. Pat co-wrote the rest, writing the wonderful first verse-introduction. Writers love their creations like they were children. I love this song. A song of redemption. A child who turned out well.

There's a storefront just off Main Street, I won it in a bet
I set up shop last August and I called the place "Regrets"
It's a name that sounds depressing,
But you don't know my story yet
Have a cup of coffee while I tell,
About the kind of service that I sell...

I used to be an artist, my canvas human skin
I tattooed tribal signs and angel wings on people then.
But I figured there's good money
Erasing youth's mistakes
Names and skulls and botched attempts
      at coiled up rattlesnakes.

<u>CHORUS</u>
Welcome to Regrets
Where mistakes are burned away
For a little pain and a lot of cash
You can leave the past to stay
I can take it off the outside but that's all I can do
Your soul, your heart and memories are up to you.

Some people knew just what they want
When they chose their art.
It sags and droops into their belts
But it still says who they are.
But some got drunk at Myrtle Beach

Didn't see the harm
Now I take off the career killers
Slithering down their arms

CHORUS
Welcome to Regrets
Where mistakes are burned away
For a little pain and a lot of cash you can leave the past to stay
I can take it off the outside but that's all I can do
Your soul, your heart and memories are up to you.

A young girl comes to see me,
Can't look me in the eye. Said
"My pimp said I belong to him
Until the day I die.
In the mirror there's a bar code
On my neck, his mark on me.
But now I've got these children,
And I'm trying to be free.

CHORUS
Welcome to Regrets,
Where mistakes are burned away
This one's on the house, dear
You can bury the past to stay
I'll take it off the outside
That's my gift to you.
All the rest from this day on is up to you

www.ingramcontent.com/pod-product-compliance
Lightning Source LLC
Chambersburg PA
CBHW052200110526
44591CB00012B/2025